Just
Eagles

Just Eagles

Text by Alan Hutchinson
Photography by Bill Silliker, Jr.

WILLOW CREEK PRESS

MINOCQUA, WISCONSIN

Acknowledgments

This book would not have been possible without the countless individuals who have given of themselves for the conservation of the bald eagle. The list includes biologists, naturalists, educators, researchers, wildlife law officers, dedicated volunteers, and caring people from all corners of the eagle's range. Without the diligent efforts of all these people, the eagle, in all likelihood, would not exist as it does today. Their efforts are truly worthy of recognition.

There are also certain people we wish to thank for the help they provided us as we worked on this book. Charles Todd, who has ably directed Maine's bald eagle recovery program for more than twenty years, reviewed the manuscript. He has also kindly mentored the author for many years on eagle biology and conservation. Ginny and Tom Chrisenton shared insights from their observations of an eagle nest near their home, and kindly allowed a passage to be used in this book.

The photographer especially thanks two people whose concern for the survival of the bald eagle obviously goes way beyond their professional duties: John White "the eagle man," a dedicated wildlife biologist with the Florida Game and Fresh Water Fish Commission, for his willingness to help me photograph the success of the bald eagle in Florida, and especially for his understanding that their future survival will increasingly require an educated citizenry, which is what this book is all about; and Kathy Hobson of the Avian Conservation Center at the San Francisco Zoo, whose cooperation permitted me to show you special photographs of an eagle hatching and of a recently hatched eagle chick that would have been unethical, not to mention illegal, to obtain in the wild.

While most of the images in this book are of wild bald eagles, the continued ability of these magnificent birds to remain free and wild is in large part due to the hard work, caring and dedication of the few people we have mentioned by name and the many we have not.

Text © 2000 Alan Hutchinson
Photographs © Bill Silliker Jr., except as follows: Alan Hutchinson pages 77, 122 and Matt Patterson pages 23 and 24(l).

Art Director: Pat Linder   Production Design: Amy Quamme/Design Solutions

Published by Willow Creek Press
P.O. Box 147, Minocqua, Wisconsin 54548
For information on other Willow Creek titles, call 1-800-850-9453

Library of Congress Cataloging-in-Publication Data
Hutchinson, Alan E.
    Just eagles / text by Alan Hutchinson : photography by Bill Silliker, Jr.
      p. cm.
    ISBN 1-57223-277-3
      1. Bald eagle. 2. Bald eagle—Pictorial works. I. Silliker, Bill, 1947-
    II. Title.
    QL696.F32 H88 2000
    598.9'42'0222--dc21   00-026390

Printed in Canada

Author's Dedication

To my family—Terri, Jon, Mom, and Dad, for all their love, support, and encouragement. And to two other people who helped guide my early life and education toward a career that has led to this book—Henry Childs and Louise Goggin.

Photographer's Dedication

To my wife, Maryellen, who kept the home fires burning—literally—while I flew off to several warm places during the height of a Maine winter to be with the eagles; for her encouragement and recognition of just how important this project was to both me and the eagles, as I logged more air miles in one year than any of the birds I photographed.

Table of Contents

The Wonder of Eagles

The dawn's light, rising on the eastern edge of the Gulf of Maine, breaks over the crest of Great Head, a landmark promontory standing near the point where the mighty Kennebec River, after draining thousands of miles of New England's woods and waters, flows into the Atlantic Ocean. The warming rays fall on a large, adult, female bald eagle. She is perched, high and protected, on a limb of a majestic Eastern white pine that first took root on that spot more than 350 years before. She has spent the night, as she has spent many before, perched in this tree that reaches close to 200 feet into the sky and whose trunk spans more than six feet across at its base.

▶ *Eagles will survey their domains from favorite perches.*

She stands sentinel in that tree, overseeing her domain, just feet from the nest that has been her home for many years and from which she and her mate have raised at least a dozen young. She perhaps was born in that nest, returning, once of age, to hatch and raise her own young from a nest that unbeknownst to her has been used by generations of eagles for a hundred years or more. Fully vigilant now, with the warming sun awakening all her senses, she scans the river below looking for her morning meal. The river is filled with runs of salmon, eels, striped bass, alewives and shad: the food that has provided for her and her brethren up and down this mighty river for centuries. Launching from her perch, rising with the warming morning air, she spies an easy catch — a ripe, roe-filed shad lazing just beneath the surface, one amongst a school of thousands. As the old eagle folds her wings to swoop upon her tasty meal, she notices the new, strange object on the water just below the river bend, downstream from her ancestral nest. She knows it is new but this large strange thing appears to be just another island, not moving, not threatening, and the eagle continues in her dive, successfully catching the fresh, full shad, coming to the conclusion that this strange new object is of no consequence to her or her kind.

Samuel de Champlain was one of the earliest European explorers to visit and chronicle the "New World" of North America. Before the Pilgrims settled Plymouth, Massachusetts, and before the Jamestown settlement of Virginia, Champlain guided his ship and crew through uncharted waters across a vast expanse of coastal lands of what would become Atlantic Canada and the United States. He traveled the mighty Saint Lawrence River, along the Coast of New England, and south to Chesapeake Bay and Tidewater Virginia.

We know from his journals that Champlain visited the Kennebec River and anchored in its mouth. It takes no stretch of the imagination to envision the eagle just described taking wing on Champlain's first morning on the mighty river and his anchored craft appearing as just another ledge.

Champlain was not only a ship's captain, master sailor, navigator, mapmaker and daring explorer. He was also an extraordinary chronicler of the world around him. How lucky we are for that and for Champlain's fascination with the new world around him — its uncharted waters, unbroken forests, magnificent rivers, and fabulous abundance of fish and wildlife, and for his

foresight and discipline to diligently record the sights before him for those at home and for those who would follow, including those of us who now follow 350 years later. His logs provide some of the earliest insights as to what this continent was like before the vast changes of settlement and the advent of our industrialized society. His writings provide an early benchmark, helping us measure and understand the monumental changes that have occurred in the world of the bald eagle and ours.

In 1605, as he navigated twenty miles up the Kennebec River, Champlain and his crew marveled at what seemed to be an endless forest of majestic pines cloaking the shores and stretching to the sky. They saw the clean cold waters of the Kennebec, one of Maine's and the continent's richest and most productive rivers, filled with salmon, bass, shad, alewives and more. The skies were filled with life: waterfowl, seabirds,

▶ *An eagle-eye view of typical nesting habitat on the coast of Maine.*

shorebirds and more, in numbers perhaps never before seen by them. And eagles: they were so abundant that early journals of the Kennebec refer to the presence of "colonies" of eagles.

Skip ahead now, about 350 years. Pollution, dams, over-fishing — all have taken their toll. The great runs of fish are all but gone. The flocks of ducks, geese and shorebirds have dwindled to a fraction of what they were. The expansive stands of old growth pines are gone as well, with just a few remaining scattered here and there. The eagles, too, are all but gone, as they are throughout the Northeast: victims as well of the drastic changes to their world.

From numbers so abundant they were once recorded as "colonial" in habit, the Kennebec's population of eagles stands at just one pair. One lone pair of eagles so contaminated with DDT and other poisons they cannot produce a chick that lives.

This pattern repeated itself in different places and in different ways across the continent. The eagles faced a dwindling supply of fish for food, were shot and poisoned as vermin, had bounties placed upon their heads, and were devastated by DDT and other chemical contaminants in their foods. Eagles suffered great declines. Concern for the bald eagle became so great it was listed under the U.S. Endangered Species Act throughout its range in the lower 48 United States in 1978.

Now take a short skip ahead, a skip in time of hope and recovery. I remember so well the afternoon when Charlie Todd, director of Maine's Bald Eagle Recovery Program, came by my office after just leaving the plane and a long, grueling day of low-level flying to monitor the health of Maine's precarious eagle population. "It's happening," he beamed. "The Kennebec is alive."

He had, that spring day in 1990, discovered two new eagle nests on the Kennebec River. A rebirth of the eagle had begun, a resurgence now being seen across its range. This book is a celebration of that rebirth and a celebration of the natural wonder we have in the bald eagle: a bird uniquely North American.

In the Presence of Eagles

The bald eagle presents a unique challenge for those who seek to photograph its life cycle. The pictures in this book include many eagles from the lower 48 United States, where the subjects were listed as either endangered or threatened under the Endangered Species Act (ESA). The ESA carries stiff fines and penalties for harassing a protected species. Making an eagle leave a feeding site by too close an approach and disturbing eagles at a nest site qualify as violations of the ESA, and with good reason. And so I had to learn when, where and how to get close enough to photograph eagles without bothering them. I also had to learn how to act to be accepted in the presence of eagles.

▼ *A Florida eagle checks its nestling.*

I partly accomplished my mission by seeking out some special places where eagles are more habituated to people.

I also sought out some special people who could help me to get closer without impacting the birds: landowners and neighbors who take pride in and provide oversight of eagle nests in their area; researchers who have made the eagle recovery programs of the ESA work; wildlife refuge personnel who have helped to provide safe sanctuaries for eagles; fellow photographers who shared information about where and when one could get close to certain eagles; and others. With their help, I was able to document the routine of an eagle family at some unique nest sites, to capture portrait images of eagles in the wild and to photograph the hatching of a bald eagle chick.

Today the bald eagle has made a remarkable recovery from the brink of extinction. As we enter the 21st century, the bald eagle is losing its protection under the Endangered Species Act. That makes it all the more important that those who seek to photograph bald eagles in the future use both care and good ethics.

The North American Nature Photography Association (NANPA) has developed suggested Ethical Field Practices for those who seek to photograph nature. They are reprinted in Chapter Six, Photographing Eagles, with the permission of NANPA. As one who helped to create those guidelines, I can say absolutely that they apply equally to watching and photographing the bald eagle, both today and in the future.

And so I urge aspiring eagle watchers and photographers alike to read this book with care to learn as much as possible about eagles and their behavior before setting out to be in the presence of eagles.

CHAPTER ONE

Bald Eagles at a Glance

If ever you have the chance to be with people when they are near a bald eagle, whether a close encounter at a national wildlife refuge or in a classroom of lucky children when a captive eagle visits with a conservation educator, watch the people's eyes. Especially watch the children. First you will see rapt attention and then you will see wonder. You will see their faces fully alive with all their senses focused on the wondrous bird sitting before them that is often looking just as intently at them! You know it is a moment that few of

◄ An Alaskan eagle warns others not to get too close.

them, regardless of age, will ever forget.

That sense of wonder reflects a special connection between people and this magnificent wild creature: the bald eagle. What is that connection? What is the mystery? What is the root of the special feelings we feel towards this majestic bird? A bird symbolic of so much: the symbol of a nation; the symbol of freedom; the symbol of wilderness and of wild places fast disappearing; a symbol of loss, imperilment and a changing world; and perhaps a symbol of hope and recovery. All those things and more shine through our eyes when we are fortunate enough to be in the presence of an eagle.

Our fascination with bald eagles also drives us to want to know more about them. Here, in brief, are answers to many of the most commonly asked questions about them.

Is the Bald Eagle the only eagle found in North America?

Two species of eagles call North America home: the bald and the golden eagle. We share the golden eagle with the world. Its range spans the Northern Hemisphere and may be the widest ranging eagle on the earth. The bald eagle, on the other hand, is our very own. It is unique to North America, found nowhere else but here.

▶ *Top: With its brown feathers, the immature bald eagle (shown here with an adult) is frequently mistaken for the golden eagle. Right: The rich colors of a golden eagle's plumage are distinctive at close range.*

Why is the Bald Eagle sometimes called a "Sea Eagle"? Scientists categorize the eagles of the world into different groups, based on how they live. One group is the Sea Eagles, sometimes called Fish Eagles, named to reflect their nature of living by the sea or other large expanses of water and feeding primarily on fish. The bald eagle falls within this group. In fact, the bald eagle's strong relationship to water defines it more than any other trait.

What does its scientific name mean? The bald eagle's scientific name is *Haliaeetus leucocephalus*. *Haliaeetus* is Latin for sea eagle. *Leuco* translates as white or clear, and *cephalus* means head. The bald eagle is then, our white-headed sea eagle.

When do bald eagles get their white heads and tails?

Young bald eagles have feathering that is brownish flecked with white from head to tail during their juvenile years. They typically gain the full white head and tail of maturity in their fifth year. This transition happens gradually, with three and four-year old eagles having increasing amounts of white blended with the brown on their heads and tails.

Do eagles look different in summer and winter?

No. Bald eagles look the same in all seasons of the year. Eagles, like all birds, replace their feathers over time. Old worn ones drop out and new ones grow in. Bald eagles, unlike many birds, do not replace all their feathers each year, but do so gradually over two, sometimes even three years. The feather molt of some birds also gives them different colored feathers in different seasons. In eagles, the colors remain the same throughout the year.

What other birds might be confused with a bald eagle?

For a full adult bald eagle, there can be no mistake. The full white head and tail against its dark brown wings and body are as distinctive as can be. One bird you could be fooled by is the osprey or fish hawk, not an eagle at all. The way to tell these two apart is by how they hold their wings in flight. The osprey's wings are swept back, giving the bird the appearance of an arrow. The eagle's wings are straighter, appearing more as a cross. Immature bald eagles can also be confused with golden eagles. Look for the golden's feathered legs and its smaller hawk-like beak and head to tell them apart. The head and neck feathers of an adult golden eagle also have a distinctive golden-bronze sheen that gives the bird its name.

How big are bald eagles?

Bald eagles are more than three feet long from the tip of the beak to the end of the tail. Weight can range from 8 to 15 pounds with females generally weighing more than males, and birds from northern populations typically weighing more than their southern cousins. Wing span may be their most impressive measure of all. The wings of a large bald eagle can span more than seven feet from tip to tip. This is second in size to only the California condor among all North American birds.

How long do eagles live?

Bald eagles have lived for over 40 years in captivity. On average, however, adult eagles in the wild have a life-span of about 15 years. Like all species of wildlife, the mortality rate of young in the first year is extremely high.

Can you tell males from females?

The male and female are similar in appearance. Both have white heads and tails as adults. But like all raptors, females typically are larger than the males, with males averaging about 20 percent less. The largest females may weigh up to 16 pounds, while males rarely weigh more than 10 pounds. This difference in size, however, is hard to notice unless the two are perched side by side.

Do bald eagles mate for life?

Bald eagles are normally monogamous, having but one mate at a time, and once a mate is chosen, the two usually remain a pair until one of them dies. When a mate is lost, the remaining bird will find another mate and form another lasting bond. As in most things in nature, there are occasional exceptions to those rules.

How old are bald eagles before they mature and mate?

Adulthood and sexual maturity are reached by bald eagles when about five years old. A few, particularly females, may mate at a younger age. In areas with large eagle populations and many established pairs, first nesting by young birds may be delayed, even though they are reproductively capable, due to difficulty finding and defending a new nesting territory.

When do bald eagles nest?

Spring is the typical time of courtship for bald eagles. And mated pairs court anew each year, even if they have been together many years. The time of year when bald eagles begin to nest varies throughout the species' broad geographic range. In the northern part of their range, eagles are often incubating full clutches by the end of March, a time when freezing rains and spring snowstorms frequently occur. In the far southern reaches of the bald eagle's range — Florida, Texas and Mexico — the nesting season is reversed, with courtship beginning in the fall and nesting through the winter. This seasonal switch seems timed to coincide with peaks of food abundance, or it may allow the newly hatched chicks to avoid the summer's potentially fatal heat.

Where do bald eagles build their nests?

Bald eagles always build their nests near water. It is a necessity for their way of life. They typically build their nests in trees, although some populations (parts of Alaska and coastal islands of California for example) build nests on cliffs. Eagles seek places for their nests that are near sources of food (usually fish) and are safe from predators and human disturbance. Interestingly, an increasing number of eagles are showing a willingness to nest near people in certain situations. Whether or not that is good for eagles, only time will tell.

How big is an eagle's nest?

A first year nest is about three feet across and one foot from top to bottom. Eagles will return to the same nest year after year, and each year add new sticks to the nest. In this way, the nests can grow to monumental size. They often measure five or six feet across, three or four feet top to bottom, and would easily support a person's weight. Built of sticks up to four feet long, the nest is more of a platform with a top lining of finer, softer material. The world record may be either a Florida nest or a Maine nest, both of which measured nine feet across and 20 feet tall, from base to top. These mammoth nests result from perhaps a hundred or more years of use by eagles. They can weigh more than two tons and their weight can eventually cause the tree to break or fall.

How many young do eagles have?

Bald eagles typically lay two eggs, although sometimes one, sometimes three, and very rarely four are laid. Two to three days typically separate the laying of each egg, resulting in a gap of days between the hatching of each chick. In some years, a pair may lay no eggs at all and raise no young. Natural events or, sadly, human disturbance can be the cause.

Which parents incubate the eggs?

The male and female stay together through the nesting season and share the duties of incubation, although the female bears most of this task. Incubation lasts on average 35 days. Both adults share the duties of raising young and both form strong ties to their nesting sites.

How fast do chicks grow?

Weighing just three to four ounces when they hatch, young eagles will increase in weight forty fold or more, to nine to fifteen pounds in less than three months time. The chicks are the size of full-grown adults by the time they fly.

When do chicks leave the nest? Eagle chicks stay in the nest until they are able to fly, about 10 to 12 weeks after they hatch. They will then spend up to six more weeks in the vicinity of the nest before departing. They then wander independently until a mate is found four to five years later.

Do eagles really have extraordinary vision?

The eagle's eyes are specially evolved to give it extraordinary vision. The eye's size and shape give it magnification when compared to the human eye. But most important, the eagle's eye is densely packed with the specialized cells that give exceptional vision. The wealth of these special cells and the way they are arranged give the eagle the ability to see extraordinary detail and observe things at great distances. An eagle can spot a fish from two or three miles away!

Do bald eagles talk?

Eagles communicate with a variety of calls, although they are usually quiet and secretive birds. They call to greet their mates or other eagles and to give alarm. The most commonly heard call is a chattering screech, similar to that made by an osprey. Eagles will also utter series of sounds to each other and to their chicks that sound like clicks and clucks: hardly the type of calls one might expect from such a majestic bird.

What do eagles eat?

The diet of bald eagles is predominantly fish. This can change throughout the seasons, with birds such as ducks, gulls and cormorants often an important eagle winter food. And it can vary with different eagle populations and even with different individual pairs of birds. Eagles are adaptable, being predators, scavengers or pirates to gain an easy meal.

How many bald eagles are there?

There may be as many as 100,000 bald eagles across their range. It is difficult to estimate population numbers of wildlife. The best numbers for bald eagles come from counting active nests. In the lower 48 states, where counts are most complete, the estimate is of nearly 5,000 nesting pairs. In Alaska and British Columbia, areas of extremely high densities of eagles, there may be as many as 50,000 eagles, and Saskatchewan may have 12,000.

Are bald eagles endangered?

In 1978, the bald eagle was listed, under the U.S. Endangered Species Act, as Endangered throughout the lower 48 states except Michigan, Minnesota, Wisconsin, Washington and Oregon where it was designated as Threatened. In 1996, as a result of population recovery, the bald eagle was reclassified under the act to Threatened throughout all the lower 48 states. In 1999, due to continued recovery, the eagle's status was again reviewed and the recommendation made to remove it from even the Threatened category in the year 2000. Eagles in Alaska were never listed as either Endangered or Threatened, reflecting the size and overall health of those populations, and in Canada, only the province of New Brunswick listed the bald eagle as Endangered.

What are the greatest threats to bald eagles?

DDT and other chemical pollutants were the major cause of the population crash of the bald eagle in the 1950s and 60s. Chemical contamination, including new threats from PCB's and mercury continue to plague the bald eagle, even as it recovers. Lead poisoning from ingested lead is a problem as well, but one much reduced since the conversion to steel shot for duck hunting. Collisions, particularly with transmission wires, are a major cause of mortality in eagles. Loss of nesting habitat is a problem in some locations, but the eagle's ability to adapt to certain human activity is giving great hope.

CHAPTER TWO
Definition of an Eagle

Because eagles are a favorite topic of young people everywhere, I have visited many schools and talked to many students about bald eagles, their plight and conservation. On many of those occasions, I've had the fun and opportunity to bring a live bald eagle into the classroom with me. It's a fascinating experience for all involved — me, the students and the eagle! The particular eagle I had as my companion on these visits is a very special one named Bart. Bart is named in honor of the place he was born — a nest on Bartlett Island on the coast of Maine, near Acadia National Park.

Bart was banded in that nest as an eaglet when about six weeks old. He was next seen when found four months later, in a Pennsylvania field, badly wounded, shot by an irresponsible 16 year old boy. Although saved from near death by a team of veterinarians and biologists, one wing was damaged beyond repair. The bird could never fly again, so, sadly, could not be released back into the wild. Two young, University of Maine researchers at that time, Charlie Todd and Mark McCollough, saw an opportunity. They saw the chance to use this grand bird, now destined to a life in captivity, to help bring awareness to people of how important eagles are, and a message of how much they need our help.

Through days of constant and patient work, using tricks and tactics passed down through falconers from ages past, these two intrepid people soon built a bond of trust with this bird. Through their patient efforts, Bart soon grew comfortable sitting on the fist of his handler and began a life of visiting and educating young and old alike across the state of Maine. Now approaching 20 years old, it's estimated Bart has visited more than 50,000 children from schools across the state, imparting an invaluable message regarding eagles, conservation, and responsibly to an entire generation of Maine students.

Others in many states saw the same need for

education and undertook the arduous tasks of training other captive eagles: Doris Mager in Florida, and people at St. Paul Minnesota's Raptor Center to name but a few. All spent untold hours and dedication to bring the message of eagle conservation to young people across the eagles' range.

Bart's presence in a classroom would always insure the students' rapt attention and would generate the most intense and provocative questions. For whatever reason, questions of what an eagle eats and how it gets its food always seemed to take center stage. In one particular classroom, rather than just give that answer as I had done many times before, I decided to turn the students into biological detectives and turned the question back on them. I challenged them to look at this creature before them and see what they could tell about how it makes its living by how it is designed.

A fascinating discussion ensued, led by that roomful of now inquisitive and probing fourth grade minds. With little hesitation, they solved the mystery and identified the two key things that make an eagle an eagle: its eyes and its talons. Those are the features that truly define an eagle and its place in the world. Other parts and senses, its hearing and sense of smell for example, contribute to an eagle's being, but they are minor in comparison to the two major features. And those young and curious students recognized

compare to the creative forces of nature that led to a creature like the bald eagle, might be the creative forces I had just witnessed in those nine-year-old minds, as they pieced together the puzzle of just what an eagle is.

The Eye of an Eagle

Eyesight is the most keenly developed of all the eagle's senses, and the one depended on most by the eagle to survive. They use their vision, above all else, to find their food. Hearing and smell are of minor consequence to a hungry eagle.

Picture how an eagle gets its lunch. A fish swims just beneath the water's surface, quietly at the edge of a marsh. Its security from predators is its coloration. It is dark on top to blend in with the water's surface when viewed from above. The fish is all but invisible in its camouflage. An eagle, riding a river of wind a thousand feet above, somehow spots this fish far below. It then folds its

those traits almost immediately once they looked at the bird with a critical eye.

A wonderful discussion then followed about the details of each of those traits and how they served to make the eagle such a master of its world. As beneficiary to their discussions, I left that classroom with a newfound sense of amazement at how natural forces and evolution had engineered the eagle into a creature so perfectly designed to fill its niche. I also left that classroom realizing that perhaps the only thing that might

wings and drops into a diving glide targeting the prey below. Exceeding 50 miles an hour as it drops across a quarter mile of sky, it must keep precisely aimed at its target. When just inches and a split second from crashing into the water, it must precisely and instantaneously adjust its flight, extend its feet and talons, and while in full flight and with perfect timing, focus on the speed and direction of the swimming fish and make perfect contact, striking the startled prey. In an act of perfect coordination it sinks and closes its talons at the precise time and place to stun or kill its prey and carry it away.

That routine task of an eagle simply getting lunch is a feat of skill, athleticism and strength comparable to the greatest athletes in professional sports. This remarkable feat requires not just strength, but great skills of "talon-eye" coordination. It's only possible because of the eagle's extraordinary vision — a degree of visual

acuity that is difficult to comprehend.

What is it about their eyes that enables eagles to see and perform so well? The size of the eye is one thing. An eagle's eyeball is huge when compared to the size of its skull and body overall. It is almost as large as the eyeball of a human. Nature has pushed this design to the limits, with the eyes so tightly fit, eagles can barely turn them in their sockets. To see up or down, left or right,

an eagle must turn or tip its head. To aid that chore, eagles have a very flexible neck and can easily turn their heads completely around to look behind them. You'll often see eagles tip their heads in this manner.

What they gain with such large eyes is magnified vision. Like a telephoto lens on a camera, the larger eye allows a greater focal distance between the lens and the retina on the back wall of the eyeball, the spot where the visual image falls. That greater focal distance, acting like a telephoto lens, causes a slightly magnified image to be seen, greatly helping in spotting distant prey. The slight magnification is one advantage to an eagle's eyesight, but the greatest asset to the eagle's vision is the clarity with which it sees. Special nerve cells make up the retina on the back wall of an eyeball. They transmit signals to the brain from images they receive. Cone cells are the specialized receptor cells on the retina designed to

◀ *An immature Alaskan bald eagle scans the ocean for food.*

capture images that are seen. The number of cone cells on the retina and how densely they are packed determine the degree of visual acuity. The more there are, the clearer one will see.

The retina in an eagle's eye is densely packed with cone cells. In addition, there are specialized grooves along the retina, called *forveae*, that contain even denser concentrations of the cones, providing the eagle with extreme clarity of vision. The old saying about people with good vision having "eyes like an eagle" is an accurate comparison but far off in reality. No person has ever had vision that comes near to being as good as an eagle's. An eagle sees up to eight times more clearly than you or me.

What does this mean?

A football is about the size of a typical eagle meal. Most people with good eyesight would be able to see that ball laying in the end zone from a distance equal to about three football fields or 300 yards. Beyond that, it would disappear from sight. An eagle, looking at the same football (or fish or duck or heron) would still be able to see it from 32 football fields away. What this means from an eagle's point of view, is that an eagle can spot its prey from nearly two miles away. Howard Eaton, a well-known and respected ornithologist and author from New York, wrote of seeing a bald eagle spot a fish from three miles away. With vision equal to an eagle's, you would be able to clearly see a pin lying along the shoulder of the highway while driving by at 65 miles an hour.

Depth perception is one final piece needed to complete the near perfect design of an eagle's vision. Depth perception is the ability to judge

◀ *Eagles find food in the open waters below dams during winter.*

once. Cover one eye to see what monocular vision does for your depth perception and imagine trying to pull out of a dive that way at 60 miles an hour, a foot before hitting the ground while trying to grab a cheeseburger on the way!

Many birds don't have binocular vision. Ducks, geese, swans, and grouse have their eyes on the sides of their heads. With this design, they can see forwards, backwards, and to the side all at once — 360 degree vision! That's a neat trick and quite an advantage for an animal that must always be on the lookout for predators hunting it as an easy meal. But that design eliminates the possibility of both eyes focusing together on the same object and these animals cannot judge distance very well. Eagles, on the other hand, like most animals that make their living by hunting, are not as concerned with what may be behind them. They need their vision pointed forward to gain a perspective of depth and distance to aid in the accuracy of the hunt.

distance. Without extremely accurate depth perception, eagles would be hurtling into the ground, unable to judge distance, especially in those last few most critical moments at the bottom of their dives, rather than skillfully and successfully striking their meal. Depth perception is achieved through binocular vision, meaning both eyes are able to focus on the same object at

The Business End of Eagles

Without exception eagles locate their prey by sight, and also without exception, they kill their prey with their feet — their talons to be exact. As impressive and intimidating as an eagle's beak appears, it is not used for killing, fighting or defense. The beak is used for tearing or shredding food once it is caught, and as massive as it is, the beak is actually quite sensitive to touch and feel and used quite delicately by the birds.

The talons are the business end of the eagle — and impressive tools they are! Each foot has four toes, three pointing to the front and one to the rear. Each toe ends in a black, stiletto-sharp talon, up to two inches long. Each foot can close with incredible force, powerful enough to drive the talons through a person's arm, and with strength so great, two people would have a difficult time prying the foot apart if the eagle wanted it closed. These tools, the foot and talons, are highly specialized among all the different species of eagles, each designed to best suit the particular way that eagle feeds and the items it seeks as prey. With such great importance as their means to catch food and survive, it is not surprising that their feet are so specialized in design, with subtle but important differences among the eagles of the world, reflecting the different foods they eat and the special hunting styles they have evolved.

The bald eagles' feet have special pads on their soles, especially designed to hold a firm grip on the slippery, wriggling fish they catch. These

◄ Talons ready, a mature eagle joins others at a communal feeding opportunity in a Nova Scotia cornfield.

sure-grip pads are found in all the sea eagles of the world — the bald eagles' cousins — which all evolved to catch and eat fish.

Powerful tendons extend down the legs and across the toes of eagles. As soon as the prey is felt by the foot, it snaps shut, sinking the talons deep in place and locking tight if the eagle wants to lift the prey, or releasing just as quickly if the eagle decides to fly by, perhaps to dive and strike again. When eagles are injured and people need to capture them to help, the first lesson learned is to control and protect themselves from the eagle's talons. There are many a poor biologist, warden, and animal rehabilitator who still bear the scars from painful encounters with those pointed talons. As sharp and deadly as those talons are, it is most remarkable how little damage eagles do to one another, even by mistake. A mated pair of eagles will touch and grab each others' talons while in full flight, yet come away unscathed.

Parent eagles walk about their nests containing tiny young, yet do no damage to the chicks. Their care and dexterity with these razor-sharp tools illustrate again just how coordinated and athletic eagles are.

CHAPTER THREE

How to Find Eagles:
Their Haunts and Habitats

Every pair of eagles has its special places —
those places where it nests and roosts, where it
hunts and feeds, and where it spends the many
different seasons. Those places hold great value
for each particular bird. They also hold great
value for those of us who care about eagles and
like to seek and see eagles in the wild. There are
certain, very special places that act as eagle
magnets, drawing dozens, hundreds, sometimes
even thousands of the birds. Those sites, dotted
here and there across the eagles' range, serve

specific and important functions for the birds,
but also serve as theaters for eagle watchers like
you and me.

The trick to finding eagles is to find those
places that are eagle magnets, and learn how you
can enjoy their use while not disturbing or
disrupting the eagles.

Before proceeding further, an important point
needs to be discussed: the great potential damage
you can cause when too close to an active eagle's
nest. The nesting season is an extremely sensitive

time for eagles and the time when your presence — any human presence — can cause great harm. This season of establishing nests, incubating eggs and raising young is the time when eagles are most vulnerable. Your presence could cause the pair to abandon their nest or you could cause the young to die. There are safe and proper ways for you to spend time with eagles during these critical times but it must be done in the right places and with care and understanding. This book gives you the information to do just that. The chapter on how to approach and photograph eagles is an essential companion piece to read with this chapter. Together, they will help you find and watch eagles in a conservation-minded way.

Keeping that important point in mind, here are a few hints to improve your chances of finding eagles in the wild. As you begin your search, key things to remember are that eagles live within a certain geographic range and that they move

within that range depending on their age and the season of the year. Remember also that they may seek out different types of habitats, those eagle magnets, with the changing seasons. And keep in mind that they will spend their time within those places in certain ways, dictated by their needs, their behavioral traits, the weather and the unique features of the place.

Your knowledge of those four things — 1) the eagles' geographic range; 2) their travels through the seasons; 3) the habitats they need and seek; and 4) how they behave in each — will aid you in finding eagles to enjoy. Knowing when and where to look is the key to success in finding eagles. This book gives you the information to help you piece that puzzle together, and as your knowledge and understanding grow, so will your chances of finding eagles and your appreciation of what you see.

The Eagles' Range

The bald eagle lives and nests successfully in a wider range of places and climates than any other bird in North America. Eagles nest from above the Arctic Circle to semitropical mangrove swamps of South Florida and arid desert shores of Texas and Baja, Mexico. This is a climatic and geographic span of three thousand miles. To the west, they nest on Alaska's Aleutian Islands just a few wing beats away from Russian soil, and fully span five thousand miles east across the continent to the Atlantic shores of Newfoundland, Nova Scotia, Maine and Chesapeake Bay. Across this area the bald eagle has adapted to almost every water-side situation where food and nesting opportunities are present.

Bald eagles are also somewhat unique in that their wintering range does not extend beyond the range of where you find them nesting. Most migratory birds have winter ranges far outside their nesting range. Not bald eagles. Eagles from the northern part of the range typically do not winter further south than the areas of Florida, Texas or Mexico where other populations of bald eagles nest. Keep in mind, however, that eagles are not distributed evenly across this broad geographic range. They are clumped and concentrated, typically in areas offering ample food and open water. Some states and regions within that broad range are thus nearly devoid of eagles, and, unfortunately, past population declines have caused their total absence from areas they once inhabited. Use that knowledge in your search for eagles.

Nesting Habitat

The eagle's nest is the center of its life for a large part of each year. Their nesting territories are frequently the places people look for and see eagles. When near nesting areas, however, it is

essential to remember how vulnerable eagles are during the nesting season. Always view the birds from a safe distance to avoid disturbing them. Never approach closer to an eagle's nest or to eagles in their nesting territory than the nearest point of existing human activity that the eagles already accept, and never behave differently than

the accustomed activities of the area. For example, if a nest occurs near a road and the eagles show comfort with cars, then you should watch from your car. Don't get out. Or perhaps you have found one of those unique situations with a pedestrian walkway that the eagles are comfortable with. If so, use it but do not stray from it. Blend in and stay within the types and patterns of human activity the birds seem to accept.

Until just recently, few nesting eagles showed tolerance of people within one-quarter mile of their nests, with nest abandonment and failure a sad but frequent result of people intruding into that sanctum. For safe eagle viewing and photographing, always follow the quarter-mile rule.

As eagle populations grow and eagles nest nearer to people, the number of people-tolerant pairs of nesting eagles is increasing. This

fascinating change on the eagles' part is increasingly common in Florida, the Northwest coast around Puget Sound, and the Maryland and Virginia shores of Chesapeake Bay. This trait may prove good for eagles, allowing increased nesting opportunities in an otherwise crowded world. However, only time will tell if being that close to people actually places them in harms way. If they succeed in more populated places, it will be good for eagle watchers by giving great opportunities to observe nests and families of eagles without placing them at risk. These are the nests to seek out as you look for eagles during the nesting season. And once found, work with the local landowners, communities, schools and conservation groups to insure they remain safe and intact for eagles and future eagle watching.

The clumped distribution of bald eagles across the range is truly pronounced during the nesting season. Nine states (Florida, Minnesota, Michigan,

Wisconsin, Washington, Oregon, Maryland, Virginia and Maine) account for 80 percent of the nesting bald eagles in the lower 48 states.

Migration

Spring and fall, especially the fall, offer great opportunities to observe eagles as they migrate between their summer nesting homes and winter haunts. But not all eagles migrate. Those nesting in places that offer ample food through the winter months will stay tied to their nesting sites throughout the year. However, many eagles are not that lucky, nesting in cold climates that freeze hard for the winter months. These birds must move each fall in search of food and open water. Juvenile and unmated eagles not yet tied to nesting sites are also natural wanderers and join in the major journeys in the spring and fall. These seasonal rhythms of eagle travels offer great opportunities for those knowing how and where

to look to witness eagles on the move.

Although there is a chance, if very lucky, to spot a bald eagle almost any place across the continent during fall or spring migration, certain places hold the highest chances for you to see these birds. These are locations that, due to their geography, shape or long, typically north-south shorelines, serve to funnel large numbers of flying eagles through a narrow spot. The Appalachian Mountain chain functions this way each fall, as wind currents rising from its flanks and the steady fall winds blowing from the north carry migrating bald eagles, along with thousands of hawks, on their southern journey. Certain locations along this chain serve as even tighter funnels as the birds ride the most favorable wind currents. Pennsylvania's Hawk Mountain and North Carolina's Grandfather Mountain are two of the most famous but there are many similar places scattered along the Appalachians and other

mountain chains throughout the eagles' range. Seek them out and you will be rewarded with a spectacle of high-flying migrants each year.

Major rivers and coastal shorelines, including the Great Lakes, provide natural barriers and act as funnels for migrating eagles. The Mississippi River may be the continent's ultimate corridor for bald eagles, both during migration and winter months. New Jersey's Cape May, Chesapeake Bay's Eastern Shore and the Great Lakes' shores also function in this way. They provide great opportunities for viewing eagles, often flying high. There are hundreds of places such as these across the eagles' range just waiting for you to discover them.

Winter and Migration

Food controls the lives and travels of eagles through migration and the winter months. To find eagles in winter, look for places with concentra-tions of eagle food: especially ducks, geese and fish. Ducks and geese migrate and concentrate in winter as well, seeking places that provide them the food and shelter they need. They often gather in spectacular numbers, with hundreds of thousands sometimes at one place. Certain species of fish migrate with the seasons as well. Huge runs and schools of fish can concentrate at mouths of rivers, on spawning beds or below dams. Any place with these concentrations of

▶ *Eagles seek out places where migrating birds, like these snow geese in Missouri, congregate.*

ducks, geese, fish or other potential eagle foods, act as magnets to eagles, especially during migration and the winter months. These are the places to key your searches. You will find that the eagles and their prey often coexist at the sites in a tense harmony that provides fascinating opportunities for wildlife viewing and study, day after day and year to year. State and national wildlife refuges are ideal places to look for eagles

in the winter months. In contrast to their need for privacy from people when nesting, eagles tend to mingle more with human settings in the fall and winter. Concentrate your hunts on large rivers and coastal waters, and always remember to ask for landowner permission when on private lands.

In General

Several things can improve your skills at finding eagles. The first is to learn as much as you can about the ways of eagles and how they view the world. Seek out and talk with people and groups near your home who may already have local knowledge about eagles nearby. Nature clubs, outing clubs, state, federal or local wildlife refuges, Audubon chapters and other bird watching groups are excellent places to make contacts with people who are always willing to share information with others interested in eagles and conservation.

Guides to wildlife viewing areas, specific to

each state and province, are becoming more

available. Look for ones covering the areas where

you live or visit. They give very good advice about

where to find various kinds of wildlife, including

eagles and other birds, especially waterfowl, which

are always an attraction for eagles. Keep in mind

too that those guides may not list all the places

◀ *Staying in or beside a vehicle and using a long telephoto lens can sometimes get photographs like this one, taken with a 500mm lens, without alarming the eagle.*

you can find eagles and often may not even list the best. This is because of the vulnerability of eagles in the nesting season, because of the wishes of some private landowners, and because wildlife managers do not want to overwhelm any sensitive areas with too much human traffic. Your quiet searches may discover some of these spots, and your conservation-minded approach to eagle viewing may open up these hidden opportunities.

Utilize topographic maps and coastal charts to refine your search to the areas where you believe eagles may live. Those sources for the United States and Canada will give you information on the location of water bodies and of such attributes as their size, shape, depth, shoreline character-istics, and degree of human development or degradation. Then use the knowledge you gain

from this book and other sources about the habitat requirements, needs and behavior of eagles and their food, and apply it to your maps and new found information of your area of interest. Build a list of the locations where you feel eagles would most likely be found. Begin to visit and explore those sites and learn from what you find. Talk to others and fine-tune your search. Don't be surprised or discouraged not to find eagles, but learn from that as well. It often takes multiple visits to a site inhabited by eagles to make that first contact and verify their presence. Ask yourself why you find them in some locales and not in others. What patterns begin to emerge from what you find? The answers will help guide you in future searching. Continually build on the foundation of what you learn.

So look, explore, and learn about the areas around your home or where you visit. Build your own information about the best sites and build

relationships with those who own or manage those sites. Eagles are habitual in the use of the areas they choose. Once you have found a location with eagles, you can almost be guaranteed to find them there later in that season or during the same season in following years. Once you have found these special locations, they can provide hours of fascinating entertainment for you, year after year. Then build your knowledge of how best to view and photograph eagles at these sites. Most importantly, however, build a relationship with the landowners around the site and work with them and the state and local conservation groups towards the care and protection of the site.

CHAPTER FOUR

The Family Life of Eagles

The Nest

An eagle's life revolves around its nest, and special is that place an eagle picks as home. Just how special that place called home can be is shown by a fascinating event in New Hampshire. New Hampshire lost its bald eagles during the widespread and tragic crash of the eagle populations of the 1940s, 50s and 60s. The last pair of nesting bald eagles disappeared from the state in 1949. For decades, New Hampshire had no nesting eagles and the stately old white pines, formerly their homes, stood stark and empty.

Remnant populations of nesting bald eagles survived nearby, with about 25 pairs in Maine to the east, but just one or two in New York to the west. These few surviving birds became the nucleus for the eagles' recovery in the north-eastern United States. As their numbers began to grow, with help from reintroduction programs in New York, Massachusetts and Pennsylvania, pioneering pairs of eagles looking for new homes began to radiate from those populations. And to the joy of everyone in New Hampshire, a pair of bald eagles again nested in that state in 1989, exactly forty years after the last pair disappeared.

As exciting as that event was, the truly remarkable part of the story was where those pioneering birds chose to make their home. After forty years of absence, this first pair of eagles to return chose not just the very same lake by which to nest as did the last pair, forty years before, but they chose the very same tree! And most remarkable of all, after four decades of winter storms, neglect, and winds, not a single stick from the earlier nest remained in that old tree to serve as a clue or magnet to these young, prospecting birds. Without any nest to attract them, without adult birds to guide them, and without any knowledge of the place, having been hatched and raised far from there, and with all the trees on all the lakes in all of New Hampshire to choose from, they chose the very place used by

the last pair forty years before. That special place held allure to this first returning pair that only an eagle could discern.

This nest site, New Hampshire's first in many years, is on Lake Umbagog, on the Maine / New Hampshire border and is now part of the Lake Umbagog National Wildlife Refuge.

How humbling and inspiring an experience that event is, to see how little we know, and how astute and intelligent these magnificent birds truly are. What did those eagles see that led them to choose that site as the premier location to build their nest, raise their young and defend against other eagles soon to follow?

Although our knowledge is far from complete, we do know much of what an eagle needs and looks for in a nesting site. Above all else, the eagles need places to build their nests. For bald eagles, this is typically tall, strong trees. The nest site must be taller than its surroundings, for the eagle seems

▶ *This pine met all the requirements of a good nest tree for this Southern bald eagle.*

to like a vantage point for watching over its realm and it needs clear flight lanes for flying to and from the nest. The tree must be strong and solid to hold a nest that can grow in size to weigh more than a thousand pounds. There also needs to be a clear line of flight through the branches to the nest, and nearby perches are a must as spots to rest, roost and feed.

White pines, giants of the eastern forest growing to 200 feet or more and once the source of masts for sailing ships around the world, are the favored choice of eagles in the Northeast. Moving westward the choices change, with cottonwoods preferred. Great Lakes' birds use white and red pines for their nests. Elms were once sought by eagles, until their sad loss to Dutch elm disease. In the South, cypress, loblolly and other pines are used. On the Pacific coast and north throughout Alaska, eagles nest in pines, spruce, firs and cottonwoods.

In nature, exceptions always seem to be the

nest in the coastal mangroves of the Everglades not many feet above the sea.

In all these situations, including the exceptions to the rules, the nest sites always provide freedom from predators and clearance for flight above the surroundings. The exceptions provide a valuable insight into the eagles' world. Consider that these exceptions (cliffs, low mangroves, etc.) are limited to certain geographic populations of bald eagles. But in those populations, these exceptional choices of nest sites become the rule. For example, populations of bald eagles that nest on cliffs rarely build nests in trees even when present. And outside those areas, it is rare to find bald eagles nesting on a cliff, even though suitable sites occur. Eagles appear to imprint on the type of nest site where they were raised, returning to similar sites when they mature and mate. In this way, these unique populations with exceptional tastes in nesting sites perpetuate the species. How they first

rule, and this holds true with bald eagles in their choice of nesting sites. At the far northern edge of the bald eagle's range, beyond the limit of trees — Labrador and the Aleutian Islands of Alaska for example — they may build their nests on the ground, typically on a cliff or ledge, again seeking sites with height and strength. This cliff-nesting behavior is also seen in eagles nesting on some coastal California islands. Another exception can be found in Florida's southern tip where eagles

began is an interesting point to ponder, but that adaptability has allowed the bald eagle to nest across a wider range than any other species of bird in North America.

A nearby, plentiful source of food is essential for a nest. Fish are most often sought. An ample supply must be available when young are in the nest. There are areas with an abundance of food at the wrong time of year, such as fall and winter runs of fish, but with little during nesting time. Such places hold little value to a nesting eagle needing to feed their hungry, growing young. Sue Livingston, a biologist studying eagles at the University of Maine, found that eagles chose which freshwater lakes and rivers to nest by based on several things. Abundant populations of species of fish that live in shallow, warm water or near the surface were one key. Catfish, pickerel, suckers and eels were preferred. Lakes with only cold-water loving game fish that live in the cool, inaccessible depths were avoided. She found that eagles also chose lakes with the most shallow water. All these things make great sense from an eagle's point of view. They make life so much easier for a bird that fishes for its living. Information from studies like this provide the foundation for programs protecting important eagle nesting areas and is leading to the bald eagles recovery and long-term health.

Privacy and safety are essential to nesting eagles. They must feel safe from predators and people. This aspect of their nesting life is one of the most interesting of all, in that the amount of human activity they tolerate seems to be an individual trait, varying from bird to bird.

Without doubt, disturbance by people causes eagle nests to fail. But the time and type of actions that cause the birds distress are different

◀ *The decision to nest beside the tennis court at this Florida apartment complex meant these eagles were extremely tolerant of human proximity.*

from place to place, so the reasons are not always clear. Eagles tend to be intolerant of human activities within a quarter mile of their nests. Closer activity may cause nest abandonment and the subsequent death of unattended chicks.

Yet there are some eagle pairs that nest near highways, malls and homes. The explanation seems to be that the eagle, as a species, can adapt in certain situations and young eagles seem to adapt much better than the older, more established pairs. Young, pioneering eagles in search of

nest sites may be forced to try new nesting sites that are less secluded than ones their parents would tolerate. If successful in raising young they will continue to nest in that place, returning each year. Their young, raised close to people, will themselves show a comfort with people, rarely seen before, when reproductively mature and seeking a site to nest. In this way, we might be seeing a dramatic change in the behavior of eagles as more and more nest closer to human settings.

This growing accommodation of people and our activities is readily seen in populations of eagles in Florida, the Puget Sound region of the Northwest, and Chesapeake Bay. The concern we must maintain is that the eagles will not raise young or survive as well as they should when living so close to humans. Forced to nest in less than optimal situations, these urban eagles may look fine to us, but their failures may be so subtle that they go undetected and lead to disastrous ends.

Eagles take great care in choosing their new homes and often take their time in making up their minds. An eagle or a pair will move into an area that seems to suite their needs and "try it on for size" for perhaps a year or two, before a nest is built or any eggs are laid. Think of this like a person renting before buying a house, using the time to judge if the neighborhood provides the things that he or she needs. For eagles those things are food, shelter, a solid site to build a nest, and security for themselves and their young.

The sight of eagles diligently carrying sticks

— materials to build their nests — is a sure sign they have made up their minds. No longer "renting" or just "passing through," they are now a full, territorial pair, serious about nesting and raising young.

If the site and pair are suited, nest building begins in the fall. It may continue slowly during winter, and is finished in the spring. They make their nests of sticks and dead branches. These are scavenged from the ground or even grabbed by an eagle in full flight and snapped from a standing tree. An eagle's size and strength is evident in the nests they build. The sticks they use may be seven feet long and four inches around. They are carefully laid and woven in the branching forks of solid limbs. The nest can soon grow to six or more feet across, and be strong and big enough for a person to stand atop. They build a finer, softer lining to the nest with grasses, twigs, pine needles or Spanish moss, a perfect bed for the eggs and chicks soon to come. Then they finish their chore by adorning the nest with fresh green sprigs of pine or other trees, a common practice among birds of prey. This fresh green adornment in an eagle's nest tells a keen observer the eagle nest is active, even if no birds are seen.

The two eagles share the chores of building or repairing their nest. Their common work and partnership also builds the bond between them. It is an age-old ritual, a testing of their skills, part of an ancient pattern of behavior evolved through trial and error, a part of their courtship, strengthening their ties, and if successful, leading to their mating and raising young that year.

Eagles measure how good a site is by how successful they are in raising young. Eagles will not return for long to nests where they met failure in their effort to raise young. On the other hand, a proven site will be used year upon year, with the

same pair and subsequent generations returning to the site, repairing and building onto the existing nest.

As new material is added each year to these successful nests, the nest can grow to monumental size. A famous and well-studied nest on the shores of Lake Erie in Ohio was more than eight feet across and 12 feet in height from its base to the newest layer on the nesting surface. Eagles used this giant for 36 years. When it finally fell in a heavy storm, it was estimated to have weighed two tons. The world record for a bald eagle nest may be a Florida nest that in 1947 was measured at 9½ feet across and 20 feet from base to top.

The story of another bald eagle's nest teaches more about how special these eagle sites can be. This one is on the shores of Merrymeeting Bay — a famous eagle place on Maine's Kennebec River. Huge in size, estimated at more than 20 feet tall and 9 feet across, this nest may have tied the record. It hugged the trunk of an ancient white pine and was woven through the tree's branches. It was believed to be more than 100 years old and used by multiple generations of eagles. The weight of this nest eventually grew beyond what that great old pine could hold, and it toppled in the1970s, breaking several large limbs from the pine as it fell. The site, however, was not lost. Eagles returned in the late 1980s to a different spot in the same tree.

The long history of such nesting sites is testified to as well in many Native American languages. A beautiful and useful trait of those languages was to use the site's name to describe important or valued features of a special place. These names give clues to the linkage of many sites to eagles in the past and give amazing evidence of their ancient and special nature. Is it any wonder then that so many landowners and

▶ *A cone-shaped nest fits in the tree perfectly for these Midwestern eagles.*

▶▶ *An immature eagle challenges a mature bird by offering its talons.*

conservation groups work so hard and focus such effort on acquiring and protecting the best of these places?

Their Territory

George Laycock studied bald eagles and chronicled their history and plight in his classic book of 1973, *Autumn of the Eagle*. In that book he describes an eagle's attachment to its home and territory in words worth repeating:

The nest is called the eyrie. As free as it seems, in reality the eagle is not free at all, except perhaps when young and not anchored to mate and eyrie. For the rest of its life, if it succeeds in entering the breeding population, the eagle lives in bondage, not to a mate, but to the master of both, the territory and particularly the giant treetop nest to which it has become a lifelong caretaker. Wherever the eagle travels, its home territory exerts a magnetic force drawing it back. The life of the eyrie may span the decades. If an eagle's mate dies, the survivor, still tied to the home territory is driven to travel in search of a new mate. When found, it will return to the nest, which in turn becomes master of the newest arrival. If the original one of the pair dies, the newest arrival will seek a new mate and in turn both will return to the nest neither had built, and become tied to its care and maintenance. In this way, the eyries span generations of eagles.

As important as the territory is, its boundaries are often ill defined. An eagle's territory is focused on its nest, its perches and a nearby food supply. It is this core that is defended against intruders, although the boundaries of its territory may overlap with those of its neighbors.

Territorial clashes are rare and fights are quite uncommon. Eagles declare their ownership by showing themselves for others to see. Whether perched on high snags or soaring above their homes, they can be seen by other eagles up to four

miles away. Their aerial courtship displays leave no doubt in the minds of neighboring or wandering eagles that the site has owners and they are at home!

In neighborhoods of eagles, neighbors become familiar with each other. They may even be related. And great tolerance may be shown as neighboring eagles fly past a pair's nest to places beyond. But let that bird stray too close, especially when chicks are in the nest, or let a stranger invade this guarded space, and trouble will surely break out. Physical contact and fighting are rare. Obviously, for birds armed with razor-sharp talons, it makes little sense to engage. Rather, loud calls with fast-flying rushes and aerial dives take place and more often than not, the intruder will turn tail and leave before any contact is made. But occasionally fighting does occur and eagles have

▶ *Real fights between eagles are rare; these birds share a feeding opportunity.*

been injured and killed in territorial disputes.

Most eagle pairs eventually have at least two nests within their nesting territory. Some may have five or more. The reason for this is not clear but it serves the pair well by giving them more than one option each year on where to lay eggs and raise young. Regardless of how many there are, all are within the core of the eagle's home and help define the territory they defend.

The Pair

Spring is a time of courtship and bald eagles get an early start on it. Mated pairs of eagles court throughout the year, even somewhat during winter, despite spending much time apart. The longer, warming days of late winter, with snow and ice still on the ground, trigger something within the eagles to make them cease their independent, wandering ways of winter and

brings them back closer to their nests. They spend increasing time together as mated pairs. They court anew each spring, even though they may have been together many years.

As with almost everything in nature, there's an exception to the rule of eagles nesting in the spring. In the far southern reaches of the bald eagle's range — Florida, Texas and Mexico — the nesting season is reversed. For these birds courtship begins in earnest in the fall, when their Northern cousins are just ending their annual chore of raising young, and they nest in winter. This seasonal switch seems timed to coincide with peaks of food abundance or may help the newly hatched chicks avoid the summer's potentially fatal heat.

As masters of the air, it is no surprise eagles court each other and build their nuptial bonds through flight. Their aerial displays form a ritual

of courtship extending over several months, and it seems the ceremony must proceed through all the stages to result in eggs and young. The ritual begins while the birds are still on the wintering grounds. It starts with soaring flights. They ride updrafted winds, circling, then diving and chasing their mate in what seems like endless play. Often, other eagles will join in, and these "pursuit flights," as they are called, continue as the eagles travel to their nesting territories. During these courtship chases, one of the pair will sometimes dive beneath its mate, rolling on its back, and with extended talons, the two will reach and touch in flight and roll, exchanging places.

A final culmination of the eagle's nuptial acrobatics is the elaborate "cartwheel fall." It has been seen by few but described by them as a magnificent display of flying and control and "the most spectacular of exhibitions." In this aerial dance, the mated pair flies high. Then one swoops down upon the other, and just as they are about to collide, they roll towards each other, interlock their talons, and with extended wings, fall in spirals towards the earth, cartwheeling downwards as they fall. They release their grasp, sometimes not many feet above the ground, and climb again to repeat this acrobatic dance.

The pair become inseparable now, spending many hours perched together side by side and touching often with their beaks. Mating will soon follow. It takes place while they are perched, usually near the nest, and is accompanied by a lot of eagle chatter.

The Young

Typically, two eggs are laid, although sometimes one, sometimes three, and very rarely four. Some years, too, a pair may lay no eggs at all and raise no young. This is caused by many things, some natural and some not. People too near the nest can cause the birds to fail. The nest may be blown down. A lack of food or a nasty, cold, wet spring can also cause the birds to fail and quit nesting for the year. Other times a pair just seems to take a year off for no apparent reason.

The color of the eggs is a dull white. They are plain, not streaked or spotted as in many other birds. Their shape is a rounded oval, not tapered as a chicken's egg. Eagle eggs are relatively small for a bird so large, being less than four inches end to end.

The eggs are laid as singles with a day or two between the laying of each. This time is needed for the female's body to produce the proteins, minerals and energy needed for each egg. The eggs may be laid at any time of day, although many feel that most are laid at or soon after dawn. Once the first egg is laid, it is not left unattended. The adults begin to incubate as soon as the first arrives. This staggered time of laying and initiation of incubation results in a staggered date of hatching and eaglets of unequal age sharing the same nest.

Both male and female of the mated pair share the chore of incubating eggs, but it is not an equal split. The female is most often on the eggs while the male hunts for food for both and continues defending their home. Growth within the fertile eggs is triggered by warmth and that

▲ *A brood patch permits an eagle to better incubate its eggs.*

must come from the body heat of the incubating adults. The thick and insulating feathers that serve to keep them so warm on winter days now pose a major obstacle to passing their body heat to the waiting eggs. To overcome this hurdle, each will lose the insulating feathers from their breasts, forming a patch of skin they can bare to brood against the eggs when it is their turn to incubate. This bare spot, called a "brood patch," is common among birds, but usually occurs only on females of other species.

Finding a dead or injured eagle is always a discouraging event, but discovering a brood patch on a dead eagle is a cause for even greater concern. The brood patch tells you the bird was actively nesting and that there is a nest with eggs or young, now with only one adult to feed and provide care. That is a difficult if not impossible situation for any family of eagles to endure and the survival of those young that year is jeopardized.

Bald eagles are attentive parents, a necessity when laying eggs so early in the spring, especially for pairs in the northern range. Eagles are often incubating full clutches by the end of March in Michigan, New York, Minnesota, Maine and north, a time of freezing rains and spring snows. The adults, usually the female, protect the eggs and keep them warm and alive through these potentially fatal storms. The eagle will lie almost

flat against the nest, nestled close atop the eggs, shielding them from the pelting rain and freezing snow, while the wind rocks and buffets the tree top nest.

A spring snowstorm can leave the entire nest and the incubating adult under a blanket of snow. The eggs, however, will still be safe and warm beneath the patient parent bird, snug against the life-giving warmth of the bare patch of breast, and nestled in the soft, dry nest. The female typically performs this trying duty and may stay protecting the eggs for days, waiting for the inclement weather to end, not feeding or leaving the precious eggs unprotected until the weather clears.

Incubation lasts about 35 days. The adults

begin to feel the movement of the chicks within the eggs and can hear them start to chirp and call several days before they hatch. It takes a chick up to several days to break its way free from the egg, chipping at the shell with its beak, aided by the "egg tooth," a small, somewhat pointed part of the beak. This is not a tooth at all, but a small sharp bump on the beak that quickly disappears after hatching when its job is done.

Hatching is exhausting to the chicks, for the parents do not help. For the first day or two, the newly hatched young lie weak and helpless in the nest, still warmed beneath the brooding parents. The eaglets are fully covered with a soft, smokey-white down but are so weak they cannot even raise their heads. They do not eat for the first day or two, sustained by the nutrients they carried from the egg's rich yolk sac, still attached to the chick's belly in a similar way to mammals being nourished through umbilical cords until born.

The hatching of the young brings a new flurry of activity to the nesting pair. They become more active and attentive to the new life now beneath them in the nest. Food will be delivered to the nest more frequently than before, even though the young are still too young to eat much or any of what is brought. For the first few weeks, there is at least one parent by their side almost constantly, brooding them near the brood patch to keep them warm, sheltering them from wind, rain or snow, shading them from the sun's heat, and guarding against predators such as hawks, ravens and raccoons, all of which could be fatal to the helpless young.

This is a time when people can do great harm by approaching too near the nest. As people approach an eagle's nest, the adult's reaction is to fly away, leaving the young exposed and vulnerable to the cold, wind, rain, burning sun, predators and other dangers around them. Even though the people causing the problem may love eagles, their inappropriate presence can result in the death of young eagles.

Stopping these mistakes and preventing the loss of young is a major need in eagle conservation and an important part of eagle recovery programs throughout the eagle's range. A growing number of wonderful success stories are being reported where people, especially those who own lands where eagles nest, are learning how to live with eagles. They are able to balance their

activities around the nest sites with the eagle's needs during these critical nesting weeks.

Home Life

Weighing just three to four ounces when they hatch, these young birds will increase forty fold or more in weight in just three months, testing their parents' ability to provide food and round-the-clock care.

By their second or third day, the newly hatched chicks have regained strength enough to feed. They have voracious appetites. Through these early days, either adult but typically the male, delivers food to the nest while the mate broods and guards the young. The favored food for bald eagles at this time is most often fish. Preferences, however, do vary and certain pairs of eagles will specialize in catching other foods. Birds such as gulls, cormorants and herons make up the primary diet at many coastal eagle nests.

Food is carried whole to the nest in the talons. For the first few weeks, the adult birds tear off small pieces with their beaks and pass them to the chicks. The pair may even share this job, one tearing bits of food and passing them to their mate who then gently presents it to the young. In the early days, the parents place the small bits of food in the eaglets' mouths. They then progress to holding the food close by, making the young reach and grab the food, then advancing to laying the scraps of food on the nest, forcing the young to pick it up themselves. In this way, the young gain coordination and start to learn to feed themselves. Both male and female of the mated pair are caring and cautious parents. To protect the young from accidental injury from their razor-sharp talons, the adults close their feet and talons while in the nest and walk on "balled up" feet around the young and eggs, cautiously and gently moving about to feed and brood the young.

When about two weeks old, the young begin to feed themselves by tearing bits of food from the meals brought by the parents to the nest. With their dates of hatching separated by one to three days, there is often quite a difference in size and strength between siblings in a nest. This difference is most noticeable in the first few weeks. The first-hatched, older bird is stronger than the others and is the first to get the food, and

◄ A patient eagle watcher might glimpse a young eaglet when it sticks its head up.

if food is scarce, will get the most. Occasionally, in times of severe food scarcity, the weaker chicks will not survive. That is nature's unremorseful way of ensuring the highest probability that at least one young eagle will be raised that year to help perpetuate the species.

In some species of eagles, sibling rivalry is so strong it is not uncommon for the strongest chick not only to out-compete its siblings, but to kill or push the weaker ones from the nest. That trait is not strong with bald eagles and is more common in many other eagle species throughout the world. When such "siblicide" does occur, it seems to happen in the first few weeks and most commonly in times when food is scarce and the survival of all is most precarious.

As the young birds grow, however, their interactions with each other grow as well and most often turn to play. The precarious nature of life for these young birds and the rough yet touching nature of that play is illustrated quite well in a story told to me by Ginny and Tom Chrisenton. Ginny and Tom have the great fortune to live in a house on an isolated island with a picture window view of a bald eagle's nest. They have learned to share this small corner of the world with a pair of nesting eagles and in exchange, see some remarkable sights. With their permission, I share this story with you. It is one of many they have shared with me about these birds.

There were two young eaglets being raised in the nest this particular year. We quickly noticed one was stronger and dominated the other. The stronger one was always first at the food and frequently pushed the weaker one away from both the food and the attentive parents. It dominated the smaller one in all respects. One day while watching, when the eaglets were about ten weeks old, we were alarmed to witness the weaker bird fall out of the nest. Its bigger brother or sister pushed it over the edge during a bout of rough pushing and play.

The falling eaglet crashed down through the branches under the nest, tumbling while trying to grasp one of the branches flashing by. In this frantic fall, one of its feet caught in a forked branch and the poor bird became firmly lodged and dangled upside down, hanging by one leg.

We expected the stronger bird, still within the nest, to turn to the food it now had unto itself. However, to our surprise it did not, but rather stood peering over the nest at its desperately struggling nest mate.

The dangling bird struggled frantically to try and free itself, but could not reach its jammed foot with its beak and could not gain a foot hold or any leverage with its wings enough to free itself. This life and death struggle went on for half an hour, the stronger bird's attention glued to its nest mate's

plight. We knew we would do more damage by intervening, even if we could, for this drama was occurring high in a tree on a remote island across the bay. Undoubtedly, we would scare and cause the second bird to jump from the nest if we approached, and thereby cause the loss of both.

We had all but given up hope for this poor young bird when we witnessed a remarkable event. The bird still in the nest, the one that had just spent the

exhausted from its struggles. The arriving bird soon began to work with its beak at the stuck foot and branches wedged around. We couldn't quite believe that bird really understood what it was trying to do, but to our surprise the hanging eagle soon was able to struggle free, and perched there with its friend.

The two then made their way, hopping, back up to the nest. Both, in due course, grew to full and healthy size and successfully flew from the nest: two new eagles on the wing instead of only one. That event we saw could be explained as simple coincidence, and we ask ourselves if we have placed too many human emotions into what we saw. We have no doubt, though, that what we saw was a strong and mysterious bond between two eagles that transcended all we thought we knew about these magnificent birds.

past weeks bullying and tormenting its smaller mate, proceeded to do what we can only interpret as an effort to rescue its helpless friend. It carefully yet deliberately made its way, by hopping and stepping over the edge of the nest, down several branches until it reached the hanging bird, now

Taking Flight

Above all else, eagles are born to fly and as soon as the chicks first sense the wind across their nest they gain an urge to try. The days in the nest are a time to grow their first set of flight feathers that will take them far and wide, and a time to gain the size and strength they will need to fly. From time of hatch to their first flight, the young wear three coats of feathers. Each succeeding covering of feathers progresses in size and strength.

Emerging from the egg, the chicks wear a soft white, smokey-colored down. Wet from hatching, it dries quickly and provides warmth but little protection from wind or rain. While wearing this down the young are constantly brooded and sheltered by the parents. This natal down lasts about three weeks. A sturdier, thicker coat of grayish, wooly down then gradually replaces it.

With this thicker down and larger size, the growing birds no longer need constant parental care. They are left increasingly on their own, though their parent are never far away and still shelter the young at night or if the weather turns wet or cold.

When the chick is about six weeks old, darker feathers begin to appear in its down. These are the eagle's flight feathers, its first set of "grown-up clothes," beginning to show themselves. These are the feathers the eagle will wear through its first year of life.

"Feathering" is the name for this process of the young chick's coat changing from a covering of down to its first adult plumage. The process follows a set and distinctive pattern, beautifully evolved in its timing to match the needs of the growing young. Feathers first appear amidst the down on the wings and tail, yet these are the last of the chick's feathers to gain full size. Since these long feathers are not needed until the eaglets are old enough, big enough and strong enough to fly,

it seems an extraordinarily smart plan nature has evolved to delay their completion. By doing so, it allows all the food the young eat to go to building bone, muscle and the protective body feathers. Wouldn't giving full flight feathers to a half-grown eagle be like giving car keys to a 10-year-old child? The outcome would not be a pretty sight!

This time of change from down to feathers is a very active time for the eaglets in the nest and they seem to love to play. Tug-of-war with sticks or bits of bone or food is a favorite game. They also now become quite aware of the world spread out around them. They will intently watch and listen to all that passes by and are increasingly attuned and intrigued by the blowing wind.

By the seventh week, their down is nearly gone and they are newly adorned with dark brown feathers, although the long flight feathers of the wings and tail are still not fully-grown. They face the wind whenever it blows and stretch and flap their wings. They are gaining their balance and testing the lift of their growing, powerful wings. As they near the day of being ready to fly, they push their tests to the edge. With flapping wings, they leap and lunge between the nest and adjacent limbs, or with talons locked on a sturdy branch, they vigorously flap their wings and actually lift and fly. With the strength they now possess, the branch within their powerful grasp will bend and rise with their pull. Their test flights and play through the final days in the nest build strength, agility, confidence and knowledge of how to use

the winds — the essentials they will soon depend on to survive.

These last few weeks in the nest are not all fun and games. They are rather dull times for the birds. The young spend most of their time quietly perched in the nest, eating, preening their growing feathers or just lying down asleep. The parents visit

An eight-week-old eaglet tests its wings.

the nest less frequently now, perhaps just once or twice a day to deliver a meal and remove scraps of food left from earlier meals. About this time the adults stop bringing new sticks to repair and refresh the nest, as they have done up to now, knowing the nesting season's end is near.

Once the young are feathered, they are left increasingly on their own, allowing both parents to now hunt for food to feed the growing and ever more hungry young.

The first flight comes when the chick is 12 to 13 weeks old. There is no magic date for this event. It happens when the winds are right and the eaglet has reached the proper growth of size, strength and feathers. It was once thought that the adult birds always teased the young from the nest, tempting them with food. Now we know that sometimes happens, but it is not always the case. The urge to fly is strong and the young are often motivated on their own.

The first flight often starts with a bout of jumping and flapping test flights just as the eaglet has done for weeks, but this time the leap is longer, the jump higher, or the talons release the branch and suddenly it's gone — airborne, perhaps to its surprise as well as joy. These first flights must be exhilarating for the birds, even though they are not long. They usually don't go more than a few hundred feet from the nest on this first flight, but what a challenge it must be to then figure out, while turning in the air for the first time, how and where to land!

They are not always graceful on these first attempts but they usually succeed. Some birds learn quickly, others are slow, and there are some that leave the nest too soon, not ready yet for flight. These most likely end on the ground, a dangerous place, but this need not result in disaster. Using leaps and short flights, eaglets on the ground can make their way up trees or cliffs, there protected from most predators for the few extra days they need to grow. If the way is clear, the adults will find their grounded chick, bring it food and perch protectively nearby. These grounded birds, with the help of a windy day, will then commonly succeed to lift off and successfully fly away.

The first flights are a dangerous time for the young, but their flying skills and abilities to find and catch food develop fast. As they do, their independence grows. Their returns to the nest decrease day by day. More time is spent on wing or perched nearby. This even holds through the night when sheltered perches in nearby trees are sought and used as nighttime roosts. The parents continue to provide some food for another several weeks, carrying it to the young at perches now, usually not the nest. As hunting skills are honed, their dependence on parents wains and ends before too long. Eight to ten weeks after flying, the bond between the young and old is broken and these first year birds, just four months old, depart their natal homes to begin their own journey into life.

◀ ▶ *First flight!*

CHAPTER FIVE

Travels and Traditions

In the world of birds, migrations are seasonal movements back and forth between breeding and wintering grounds, locations that are most often distinct and distant places. Some species undertake truly world class journeys, migrating thousands of miles and spanning continents. Our eagles are not that ambitious. You can think of them more as travelers than as migrants, and here is why.

The bald eagle is different from many other birds in that their seasonal migrations, or travels, do not go beyond the geographic range in which this species nests. However, across this broad geographic range, there are multitudes of patterns to the seasonal travels among the many separate eagle populations. The result is a complex mosaic of movements, exquisite in design, and evolved to fit bald eagles into many different places, including environments as diverse as arctic shores and tropical coasts. Each eagle population differs slightly, each evolving to fit the nature of the lands it calls home. There is no set pattern. Some migrate north, some migrate south, some to the east, some to the west and some not at all.

All that variation seems quite odd at first and makes one wonder "why?" The answers lie in the great adaptability of the bald eagle as a species. It is able to live and nest successfully in a wider range of places and climates than any other bird in North America. For example, bald eagles nest from above the Arctic Circle to the semitropical mangrove swamps of South Florida and arid desert shores of Texas and Baja, Mexico. This is a latitudinal span of three thousand miles. To the west they nest on Alaska's Aleutian Islands and their range extends five thousand miles across the continent to the Atlantic shores. Across this area the bald eagle has adapted to almost every situation where food and nesting opportunities are present.

This tremendously broad range, unsurpassed by any other bird or mammal on the continent,

shows us just what an adaptive marvel the bald eagle truly is, for it could only succeed in using all these different climates by being able to adapt its movements and lifestyles to fit the challenges presented by each place.

Unlocking these complex mysteries of when and where our eagles travel is not an easy task. Yet, we need to know these things if we are to help the eagles recover and succeed. The many dedicated people who have worked years to solve these problems deserve our thanks for giving us the knowledge we now have.

Knowledge of the bald eagles' travels comes by marking individual birds, then hoping they are seen and reported again. Over time, these reports build a map of information linking different places with eagle populations. Banding eagles is the most common way to mark the birds. This is done by placing a special band around the eagle's lower leg, just above the foot. An aluminum band

▶ *A Washington state leg band on an eagle wintering on Alaska's Kenai Peninsula.*

issued by the U.S. Fish and Wildlife Service is always used. It is stamped with a unique set of numbers, and once placed around the eagle's leg, that number is assigned to that bird for life. A special, especially strong, band must be used to prevent the eagle from prying the band off its leg.

A second band, often color-coded or with large numbers for ease of reading from far away, is often placed around the other leg. Other colored or numbered markers may also be attached to the wings or tail to help in special studies. Only markers that have been tested and proven safe are allowed for use, and only specially trained and licensed people are allowed to catch and mark the birds.

Young eaglets in the nest are the birds most often banded, since it is so hard to capture the adults. Researchers have learned how and when to undertake this task to avoid risk to the eagles. The safest time to do this is when the eaglets are five to six weeks old. They are large enough to hold the bands or markers and are sufficiently feathered to be able to withstand the temporary absence of sheltering parents. Yet they are not so old that they may jump from the nest at the approach of people and fall to the ground below. Care must be given not to approach the nest too early in the nesting cycle, when eggs or small young are most vulnerable to wet, hot or cold weather.

A trained climber scales the tree and slowly edges over and onto the nest. The young are gently coaxed to where they can be reached, then held while bands and markers are attached. Sometimes the chicks are lowered in protective cloth sacks to researchers on the ground. This also is the time when valuable information is recorded on their size, growth and health. The birds are then gently returned into the nest and the climber slowly leaves. Banding visits are a one-time, carefully timed and planned event carried out by trained

and licensed professionals. Repetitive or ill-planned visits can be quite harmful.

Fortunately for the climber, the adults are not inclined to attack. They fly or perch nearby and watch the goings-on but, for unknown reasons, don't try to drive away the strange intruder. They will be back at the nest, however, soon after the climber leaves, checking on and caring for the young. It is a thrilling site to see this kind of work, but there is a special time and way to do it safely, and must only be done by those with training and

a license. From Newfoundland to Florida, Texas to Minnesota and Alaska to Maine, more than 10,000 bald eagles have been marked since 1935.

Included in the list of those who have worked so hard to understand the lives and travels of eagles are people like Charles Broley and Francis Hobart Herrick, pioneers from the past. Charles Broley, a retired banker, is legendary among those who study eagles. He banded more than 1,000 eaglets from nests in Florida and Ontario, and in addition to learning about the movements of eagles, it was his work that brought to light the calamity of DDT and the crash of the bald eagle population. Francis Hobart Herrick, a professor at Ohio's Western Reserve University, spent 30 years, beginning in the early part of the 1900s, studying the bald eagle. He wrote the first comprehensive book about the species' life and nesting traits, and from his work we have invaluable insights about the bird and its world before DDT.

Others now continue the work begun by those pioneers, and from the hard work of Broley, Herrick, and many others, we see a complex pattern of seasonal movements of eagle populations across their range, with each variation explained by the adaptability of this bird.

Despite the many variations, however, a few common traits still appear. One of these is that in all populations of eagles, the young birds wander far from home in their first few years of life. The newly independent young, just two or three months on the wing, disperse for parts unknown. Their journeys can take them far and in many different directions. Young from Maine are found in Nova Scotia and Virginia, while Maine may host young from Saskatchewan or New York. Minnesota birds can be found in Mississippi and young from Florida will visit the Chesapeake Bay.

The young dispersing birds generally travel south, although some first will travel north

before turning to the south and its better winter climes. The Florida birds, again, are exceptions to the rule. Florida birds, remember, are born in the cool of winter and take flight perhaps in March, reversed from most other eagles. Their travels are reversed as well; the young fly north in their dispersal, escaping the summer's heat. Traveling north along the Atlantic seaboard as far as the Canadian Maritimes, they arrive at a time when

▶ *Two immature bald eagles play as they cruise the Pacific coast.*

young eagles there are only newly hatched. The dispersing young bald eagles from populations in the Midwest, plains or mountain regions often tend to head for seacoasts or large rivers and lakes.

The second common trait of eagle populations is that food appears to be the directing force behind most eagle travels. Once an ample source is found, the young especially will linger on. It is the nature of the young, however, to travel wide and far. They may fly back by their birth nest at times throughout those years, but they continue on their way. It seems they have no set path, but an overriding, unconscious goal to explore their world and learn the skills to survive to parenthood.

Once an eagle reaches three to five years old, its independent journeys cease, a mate is found, and this wanderer becomes homebound. The home that is picked is often in the region where it was born, even the same nest if their parents are

deceased. Or, they may reside far from that home, perhaps attracted to their new mate's place of birth, or possibly, with pioneering spirits, to an entirely foreign region free from other eagles to compete against the new arrivals. Many young join with a previously mated eagle, filling the place of a mate recently lost.

Eagles lose their wanderlust once they've set up home. For many established nesting pairs, there is no migration or movement from the nesting territory. For these, everything they need is available near their nests year round. Some will only leave when they must travel to find food.

Eagles nesting in the far north of the eagle's range, such as interior Alaska and Canada, must leave in search of food when deep winter cold sets in and the feeding waters near their nests freeze. Their departure does not last, for as soon as a thaw arrives, they return with haste, if only for a few days before another freeze sets in.

There are some eagle populations that do undertake long journeys between nesting sites and their winter homes. The term migration applies in full to these long distance travelers. Eagles travel through the day and roost and rest at night. Days with strong, clear weather fronts, with steady blowing winds directed towards the eagles' line of flight, are favorites of these birds.

In the fall, strong northwesterly winds pushed by cold fronts from the north can carry multitudes of eagles from these northern grounds. The eagles seek out rising thermal currents from air heated near the ground, and ride them in great spirals until they appear as mere specks in the blue sky. They will then turn towards the south and soar along the prevailing wind, gradually descending in a glide. When that ride is done, they will catch another lifting current to repeat the feat again. They can travel hundreds of miles in a day this way, hardly flapping a wing,

geniuses at conserving energy as they journey toward their destination.

There are places along these travel routes where the rise and shape of the land funnels the winds, and therefore the birds, along narrow paths of sky. At these unique geographic junctures, hundreds of eagles may pass through during the season. Hawk Mountain in eastern Pennsylvania, high along the Appalachian ridge, is one of the most famous and spectacular of all. Each fall, people gather to witness the spectacle of eagles and hawks passing in their autumn flights. These are wonderful sights to behold and wonderful places to visit. Many parks and preserves will accommodate you with guided tours. You can contact them to learn the best dates and times for the area you wish to visit. As a general rule, bald eagles begin to move from their northern ranges in October, and the migration peaks later in November. Their return in spring begins as early as February and is done by April's end, although the spring flights to the nesting grounds are never as spectacular as the fall events.

Regardless of their wanderings, travels or migrations, eagles always hear the call from home. Whether old or young, whether on a week-long or five-year journey, and whether an established pair or newly mated pioneers, what

may seem at times aimless wanderings, all somehow end with a return to their nesting sites.

Winter's Challenge

Winter is a time of challenge for all wildlife, and eagles are no exception. It is a time when the search for food overrides all other concerns. There are three points in time during the eagle's year, bottlenecks so to say, when the eagle's fate is tested most and things are most apt to go wrong. The first is after hatching, when the adult male must hunt for all — himself, his mate and young. A scarcity of food or his poor skills can spell disaster for the chicks and result in failure to raise young that year. The second point of testing is later in the summer, when the young break the family bonds and must hunt and feed themselves. Fortunately for the eagles, food is rarely scarce at either of these points in time, reducing the risk of death.

Winter is the third and harshest test of all in the eagle's annual cycle of survival. With winter's frigid cold and scarcities of food, starvation leads to the most deaths of eagles in the wild. The youngest birds, those just on the wing, are most susceptible of all. Studies show that more than 50 percent of all the eaglets raised may not live to be adults. Winter takes the highest toll, with many young not surviving to see their first spring.

Food controls the lives of eagles through these trying winter months, so with food so scarce and important, it should come as no surprise to learn that eagles change their ways of survival during these times. If food is in abundance, they become sociable in winter in a way that helps them all. They no longer defend territories, as they did around their nests, but work together in a communal sort of way. When ample food is found, eagles start to gather around, and the first to find the meal, surprisingly, does not skulk or hide or

chase other eagles away, although numerous minor fights and bouts take place. This social nature and communal feeding, so different from the territorial behavior seen at the nests, is an adaptation for survival that works for one and all.

Food for eagles in winter is a "feast or famine"

▲ *A winter-killed deer provides a welcome food source.*

▶ *Stealing food from each other*

ordeal, for food is often scarce, but when found, can be in great abundance for at least a short time. Wintering flocks of ducks, spawning runs of salmon, schools of milling fish below a dam or carrion (the carcasses of dead animals) are the foods that often fuel the eagles through the winter. Carrion is especially important for the young. They are more dependent on such foods than adults who have learned through trials of past winters how and where to find live prey. The carcasses of moose,

deer, elk, sheep and cattle, dead from winter stress, are mainstays of many eagles' winter diet. Historically, when the great herds of buffalo roamed the plains and when whales and seals swam the seas in numbers no longer seen, the remains of their dead no doubt also played a major role as a winter food for eagles. As those animals were hunted with no controls a hundred years ago, their populations crashed and with that loss we then saw the first phase of our eagles' decline. Perhaps even now a lack of winter food limits how many eagles can survive.

Eagles gather whenever a source of food is found and stay until it is gone. This communal gathering of birds takes full advantage of the temporary source of food. When it's gone, they move on in search of the next winter meal. The birds will scatter individually in this random search for food, then when another source is found, gather once again, the first arrivals announcing, through soaring flights, the feast waiting below.

An eagle's winter life is a delicate balance between finding enough food to live and expending as little energy as possible in the effort, to minimize how much food it needs. As a result, a typical winter's day in an eagle's life is quite dull, made up of sleeping, perching and eating — mostly the first two. Nights are spent at sheltered roosts, trees or cliffs, protected from winds and cold. In places of food abundance where eagles concentrate, the nighttime roosts become communal, with sometimes dozens, even hundreds of eagles vying for the favored perches.

As the light of dawn starts to tinge the sky, the eagles leave the night roosts and fly to the winter feeding grounds. These feeding places may be several miles away. Once there, they may make a pass or two in the early morning light, hoping to find an easy meal of a dead fish or duck washed

▶ *Stealing food from each other is a common eagle trait.*

up on shore from the night before. If not, they'll land on a nearby feeding perch, there to spend the day, making short flights, now and then, when something catches their eye. When food is caught it's carried back to the perch, often amidst great commotion, as other eagles chase the successful hunter in hopes of stealing a meal.

If the food is too big to carry, say the carcass of a moose or deer on a frozen lake, the birds gather together at the carcass, feeding side by side and occasionally fighting over bits of food. They eat voraciously and gorge if food is ample, then return to perch and rest throughout the remainder of the day.

When the weather is harsh and stormy, they may not leave the sheltered roost for days, not feeding at all but conserving what energy stores

they have for tougher times to come. Studies have shown just how patient and sedentary these birds can be. Some have been observed spending up to 20 of the 24-hour winter day resting on their perches.

If the weather is clear and sunny, afternoons may find the eagles soaring on the thermal winds rising from the warming ground. In areas where eagles congregate, dozens may be seen aloft at once, enjoying a respite from the winter's hold. It is on such flights, on sun filled days as winter moves along, that bonds between mated pairs begin to form again or build anew between young birds. On these fun-filled flights of late winter days, pairs begin their aerial displays and start their courtship rites that will lead them on to home and another nesting year.

CHAPTER SIX • by Bill Silliker, Jr.

Photographing Eagles

Those who want to photograph bald eagles need to carefully consider a number of things. Not the least of these is the impact one might have when attempting to get close enough to photograph these obviously powerful yet actually quite sensitive birds.

It's worth noting again that bald eagles have not enjoyed a good experience, overall, with humans. Despite its status as the national bird, the bald eagle was persecuted for generations in many regions: people shot them, poisoned them

and otherwise harassed them. That may be why most bald eagles are so wary of humans. Some get visibly upset when they even see people. Some call out. Others fly away. These behaviors present problems for a photographer, but they should also raise caution flags.

The comments of early naturalists suggest that where eagles have not been harassed, they tolerate closer human encounters. Perhaps that's true. The eagles I photographed at several special places in Florida, Alaska and Missouri were much more

▶ *Spotting scopes and telephoto lenses make the enjoyment of eagles safer for the birds.*

tolerant of humans at a closer proximity than are most eagles in other regions.

Here are a few tips that can help you to get great photographs without causing eagles any harm. The first is to use a long enough telephoto lens, something in the 400mm range or longer. Always use a sturdy tripod under such long lenses. The use of a good quality teleconverter will extend the range of your lens. But if you don't have a quality teleconverter, don't use it: cheap glass makes for poor pictures. In camera gear, you get what you pay for.

And if you don't have a long enough lens? Don't push it. Ethical wildlife photography requires that one forego attempts to photograph wildlife if the attempt might harass or somehow place the subject in jeopardy. Be satisfied with

images that show an eagle in its habitat. Editors use those, too.

I also urge you to read and to follow the Ethical Field Practices suggestions of the North American Nature Photography Association that end this chapter.

Where the Birds Are

Many eagles overwinter along the northern tier of the United states, from Maine to Washington state, sticking it out in the cold and snow along with the best of us. The key is to consider what and where the food sources are and then go there. For example, bald eagles are showing up in ever increasing numbers along and near the Mississippi and Missouri Rivers in winter, especially in pursuit of prey species such as snow geese. Areas in several states, including Missouri, Iowa and Minnesota, have good eagle photography areas.

Eagles sometimes work downstream of dams on otherwise frozen rivers in hopes of catching a fish that might have gotten chewed up or dazed by the process or simply because it's the only open water around.

Ice fishing enthusiasts know that eagles often land on the ice to grab fish waste or discarded bait. Keeping an eye out for eagles perched in the trees along the shores of rivers, lakes and ponds where ice fishing is popular is a good idea. An ice fishing hut could also provide a good blind from which to work in some situations.

These situations usually require that you get there before the birds do and find a way to hide from them, such as by using a portable blind like a camouflage colored tent, or perhaps if you have the chance, a more solid structure made of wood. Always ask for permission before erecting any blind, and remember that it may attract others or could be trashed by vandals.

Sometimes you can use a vehicle as a blind. Window mounts and bean bags provide stable support for the heaviest of telephoto lenses when used carefully. I set up a tripod when alone in a vehicle, extending one leg to the passenger side door to hold the tripod firmly in place.

It's also no secret that many folks go to Alaska

to photograph bald eagles. As November approaches, a large gathering of bald eagles occurs at the Chilkat River in Haines, Alaska, north of Juneau. Other places in Alaska also have bald eagle concentrations during fish runs.

And if cold isn't your style, don't overlook Florida. Florida actually has more nesting bald eagles than any other of the lower 48 United States, and some of them have selected publicly accessible nest sites near golf courses!

Try typing bald eagle into an Internet search engine and you'll be stunned at what you get.

Exposure Matters

Remember that the most important part of the eagle is the head. On a mature bird, that's all white. To get enough detail in the white feathers, you need to cut back on the light reaching the film. For an immature bald eagle, which is nearly all brown, use an exposure setting for an average subject.

What's an average subject? Look for something that reflects an average amount of light and meter from that to set the exposure for a subject that's in the same light. And what's an average amount of light? Middle toned green grass reflects an average amount of light. I always carry a gray card, a piece of cardboard or plastic that's a neutral gray color, available from many camera stores, to keep a reference point available. Gray cards are designed to reflect an average amount of light, just the way an average subject or scene does.

Hold the card in the same light as the subject

average amount of light, be they trees, grass or rocks. Be careful when metering with really light or really dark elements in the viewfinder.

Practice by checking out what in nature reflects the same amount of light as a photographic gray card. Then you'll know what you can trust to meter from in the natural world. Base your exposure settings on an average reading and adjust, if need be, to allow a bit more light to hit the film for an all black dog, or a bit less light for a mature bald eagle's head.

I set exposures for mature bald eagles at a half a stop to two thirds of a stop less than what a setting for an average scene would be. For the mostly brown immature eagles, I simply use the setting determined from the gray card. The difference is in the head of the bird, where you want feather detail to show. Overexpose the all-white head of a mature eagle and you'll lose definition. Catch yours in the good light.

and meter from it. Watch out for tipping the card into the sunlight too directly or letting it fall into its own shadow. Hold it evenly in the light. Many gray cards exist in nature. The blue sky works well, not the deepest blue sky, nor the lightest, but the average blue sky that's directly opposite the sun. There's also average gray rock, average yellow grass in wetlands or along roadsides, average gray bark on some trees — the list goes on and on. Meter the elements found in nature that reflect an

North American Nature Photography Association
Principles of Ethical Field Practices

NANPA believes that following these practices promotes the well-being of the location, subject and photographer. Every place, plant and animal, whether above or below water, is unique, and cumulative impacts occur over time. Therefore, one must always exercise good individual judgment. It is NANPA's belief that these principles will encourage all who participate in the enjoyment of nature to do so in a way that best promotes good stewardship of the resource.

Environmental: Knowledge of Subject and Place

- Learn patterns of animal behavior — know when not to interfere with animals' life cycles.

- Respect the routine needs of animals — remember that others will attempt to photograph them too.

- Use appropriate lenses to photograph wild animals — if an animal shows stress, move back and use a longer lens.

- Acquaint yourself with the fragility of the ecosystem — stay on trails that are intended to lessen impact.

Social: Knowledge of Rules and Laws

- When appropriate, inform managers or other authorities of your presence and purpose — help minimize cumulative impacts and maintain safety.

- Learn the rules and laws of the location — if minimum distances exist for approaching wildlife, follow them.

- In the absence of management authority, use good judgement — treat the wildlife, plants and places as if you were their guest.

◆ Prepare yourself and your equipment for unexpected events — avoid exposing yourself and others to preventable mishaps.

Individual: Expertise and Responsibilities

◆ Treat others courteously — ask before joining others already shooting in an area.

◆ Tactfully inform others if you observe them engaging in inappropriate or harmful behavior — many people unknowingly endanger themselves and animals.

◆ Report inappropriate behavior to proper authorities — don't argue with those who don't care; report them.

◆ Be a good role model, both as a photographer and a citizen — educate others by your actions; enhance their understanding.

CHAPTER SEVEN

Eagle Conservation

Bald eagles hold a fascination for us today and similarly held a fascination for those who came long before us. The place of reverence and lore the eagle holds in Native American culture speaks to the ancient ties this wild creature has with people. And before the Pilgrims of Plymouth and before Virginia's Jamestown, European navigators and explorers, such as Captains George Weymouth and John Smith, found reason to note the presence of "gripes" — as eagles were called in the Europe of their day — in the journals of their travels. One can only imagine the world these people saw as they guided their ships and crews through uncharted waters from Canada to Florida. One can hardly imagine the unspoiled rivers and bays they saw, the waters filled with fish and food, the unbroken forest shorelines and the fabulous richness of wildlife. One feels how strong a mark the sight of eagles left on these early explorers by how clearly and regularly they mention such sightings in their chronicles amidst all else there was to report of the natural wonders and wealth of the New World around them.

There is no way of knowing just how many eagles may have lived throughout the continent when Europeans first arrived. It's clear from those early reports that the eagle's range was fully as wide then as it is today, spanning thousands of miles from Florida to the Aleutians and from Newfoundland to Mexico. Most astonishing from our vantagepoint today is that those reports also give a picture of bald eagles living on nearly every body of water across the continent. There may have been a half million bald eagles living in North America when Europeans first arrived. It was not to last.

Those early settlers viewed their new strange home as a place to be tamed and used to survive. Eagles were seen as a threat or nuisance. They were viewed as predators to be killed. They were once even shot and fed to pigs. This killing took its inevitable toll as settlements spread from coast to coast. And that toll was raised by the steady loss of nesting sites and habitat to cities, towns and farms. By mid-1800, the first major decline of the bald eagle was reported by those few people at that time who showed concern for such things. John James Audubon was one.

Bald eagles were not alone in their plight. Wildlife of all types was in serious decline from the Atlantic to the Pacific. Those were times when most people believed that wildlife was unlimited and existed to be taken to its fullest. Those were times of no hunting laws with no conservation ethic or societal sense of responsibility for the natural world. The passenger pigeon, the most abundant bird in all of North America, was driven to extinction. The buffalo went from millions to the verge of disappearing. Waterfowl, fish, shorebirds, whales, seals, elk, deer and more went from numbers termed uncountable to tiny remnant populations. All had been important

food for eagles in different seasons and in different portions of its range. The ecological repercussions of that vast loss were enormous on the natural world of North America, and directly on the bald eagle.

An enlightenment began in society as the 1900s dawned. People awoke to the fact that wildlife was not unlimited but needed to be protected. Some of the first and most significant (even to this day) national, state and international laws for wildlife conservation were enacted in response. Wildlife populations rebounded. The bald eagle was one. Its recovery was reported from many states. Unfortunately, though, this good news would not last.

Society's industrialized ways became the next challenge to the survival of the eagle. It was a monumental challenge — one that nearly caused

◄ A Southern eagle shares a favored perch tree with a cormorant and two vultures.

► A good perch doesn't always have to be a tree.

the eagles' demise in much of its range and one that continues today. The major culprit was the insecticide DDT.

Used to kill mosquitoes and other insect pests, residue from this pesticide fell to the ground, seeped into the soil and leached into our groundwater, rivers, lakes and oceans. Beyond its lethal form and level, microbes in the soil and water ingest it. They are then eaten by insects, worms and small fish, which in turn become food for larger fish, birds and mammals. The chemical

is passed along this chain of feeding, and concentrated in higher, more toxic levels with each step up the chain.

Eagles sit atop this trophic pyramid and paid a deadly price, for DDT takes its toll in a sinister way. In extremely high doses, DDT can kill an eagle, but that is rare and was not what caused decades of declines among bald eagles.

Eagle courtship culminates each spring with the laying of a clutch of precious eggs. The production of that egg is a delicate and complex physiological process within the female eagle's reproductive tract. Various nutrients, fats and proteins are layered around the now fertilized egg as it passes through the oviduct, making up the yolk, the white and essential membranes of the finished egg. The final step in this remarkably complex process is the placement of the hard, protective calcium laden shell on the outside of the egg, just before laying.

DDT and its by-products play their dirty trick by chemically blocking the eagle's physiological ability to deposit the calcium needed in that final stage. Lacking calcium, the eggshell is thin, weak and sometimes missing entirely. When the egg is laid and incubation begins, just the weight of the incubating female would be enough to break and crush the egg, and a year goes by with no young.

DDT was so widespread that reproductive failures were reported, with only few exceptions, across the entire eagles' range. In many places, reproduction dropped by 90 percent or more, with too few young to even replace older adult birds dying of natural causes. Eagle populations crashed, and they disappeared from wide areas throughout the lower 48 states. In the few pockets where they held on, few chicks were raised. Other problems added to their woes: nest sites were lost to houses, malls and roads; transmission lines caused collisions and electrocutions; illegal

shooting took on big importance with eagle numbers so low; birds were poisoned from lead ingested as shotgun pellets in dead and wounded waterfowl; and other chemical contaminants weakened the eagles' chance of survival.

At its low point there were only about 1,000 nesting pairs of bald eagles left in the lower 48 states. In 1978, the bald eagle was listed under the U.S. Endangered Species Act as Endangered throughout the lower 48 states except Michigan, Minnesota, Wisconsin, Washington and Oregon where it was designated as Threatened. Eagles in Alaska and most of Canada escaped the worst of

these declines. With that recognition, recovery programs were begun and, encouragingly, DDT was banned from sale in the U.S. and Canada.

Eagle population surveys and research increased, giving better understanding of the problems and possible solutions. Programs were started in many states and Canadian provinces aimed at recovering the eagle. Heroic efforts were tried with much success. Eggs or young were transplanted from healthy wild populations or captive flocks to nests where eggs had failed, and methods were found to make foster parent eagles accept the new arrivals. Reintroduction programs raised hundreds of young eagles in semi-captive sites and released them into the wild, leading to reestablished populations across the eagles' historic range. Wildlife agencies and landowners worked out ways to protect many of the remaining eagle nesting sites and, in places where few nest sites remained, artificial structures were

constructed to give returning birds an undisturbed spot to nest. These efforts were costly and required the dedicated efforts of many, including volunteers.

Fortunately, their hard work is paying big dividends. In 1996, as a result of population recovery, the bald eagle was reclassified under the Endangered Species Act to Threatened throughout all the lower 48 states. And in 1999, with the eagle population estimated to be approaching 5,000 nesting pairs, the eagle's status was again reviewed, and a recommendation was made to remove the bird from even the Threatened category in 2000.

The bald eagles' recent story is truly one of hope and recovery. But the longer story, made up of several cycles of the eagle riding high then low, is one of caution for us all. There are signs already that another crisis could be at hand. Mercury, PCBs, dioxin and other chemical contaminants

are found in eagles and their eggs across their range. Pockets of low or failed reproduction still plague certain areas. DDT's harmful by-products can still be measured in many eagle eggs.

We have done well in working to bring the eagle back, and eagles have done their share as well. A clear example is the increasing occurrence of eagles nesting near or even adjacent to people and our activities, a situation that was almost unheard of 20 years ago. The bald eagle has proven it is capable of overcoming challenges posed by people if we give them time and help.

The special connection between people and bald eagles of course did not start with the arrival of Europeans to North America's shores. From time immemorial, the bald eagle has held special spiritual meaning to Native American people, and that spiritual and cultural reverence continues today. The depth of that relationship is shown so clearly by how frequently remains of eagles are

found in Native American archaeological sites across the continent. And the breadth of that relationship finds testament in the multitude of Native American place names across this land referring to the presence of eagles.

From early Native Americans to today's school children, bald eagles hold a special place of reverence in our hearts and minds, spanning time and place. The eagle is a symbol of cultures, of a nation and of freedom. It is a symbol also of our changing view of natural resources and wild places: a change from a view of endless abundance with no limits to a growing understanding of the limits of our shared natural world, of our responsibility in it and its potential loss. It is a symbol of a society awakening to the knowledge that our growing population, industrial ways and pollution can have dire effects on the world around us if we are not careful. And the eagle is a symbol of hope and recovery, of a commitment by a society to understand its connection to the natural world, to value that world around us and to work to right the wrong of a species in decline. And now, perhaps, it is a symbol of success, but only time and our diligence will prove that true.